Artificial Intelligence, Real Profits:

Mastering ChatGPT-4 for Business Marketing

by Jack Pemberton

with the assistance of ChatGPT-4

Formatted, Converted, and Distributed by eBookIt.com
http://www.eBookIt.com

ISBN-13: (hardcover)
ISBN-13: 978-1-4566-4073-6 (paperback)
ISBN-13: 978-1-4566-4074-3 (ebook)
ISBN-13: 978-1-4566-4075-0 (audioebook)

Table of Contents

Introduction

Ladies and gentlemen (and AI reading this), welcome to a realm where imagination meets profitability—where the cutting-edge technologies of Artificial Intelligence (AI) intersect with the art of marketing. Get ready to embark on a transformative journey as we dive into the depths of "Artificial Intelligence, Real Profits: Mastering ChatGPT-4 for Business Marketing."

In this book, we'll unveil the secrets of leveraging AI's most impressive tool—ChatGPT-4—to supercharge your business marketing strategies. It's time to embrace the potential of AI and harness its power to drive real, tangible results.

Now, you might be thinking, "What exactly is ChatGPT-4?" Allow me to illuminate your path. ChatGPT-4 stands for "Chat Generative Pre-trained Transformer 4." It's the latest incarnation of AI language models that can engage in conversational interactions. Picture it as a brilliant virtual assistant, armed with intelligence, charm, and an unrivaled knack for understanding and responding to human language.

Throughout our journey, we'll delve into the art and science of business marketing. Together, we'll explore the transformative power of ChatGPT-4, unlocking strategies that will elevate your business to new heights.

From social media platforms like Facebook, Twitter, and Instagram to the realms of YouTube, websites, and blogs, we'll unravel the mysteries of ChatGPT-4's applicability in each domain. You'll discover how to captivate your audience, generate leads, and maximize your profits through real-life examples and actionable techniques.

But here's the best part: you don't need a computer science degree to make this happen. This book is designed with you, the ambitious entrepreneur or savvy marketer, in mind. We'll demystify technical jargon, making AI concepts accessible to even the most non-technical minds. So, whether you're a seasoned professional or a budding entrepreneur, this is your gateway to mastering AI-driven business marketing.

Prepare yourself. We're about to embark on an extraordinary journey where the realms of AI and business marketing converge. Get ready to unleash the power of ChatGPT-4 and witness the transformative impact it can have on your business success. Let's set sail towards a future of Artificial Intelligence, Real Profits.

PART I:
Understanding the Basics

Chapter 1:
Introduction to AI and ChatGPT-4

In the initial chapter of our journey, we embark on a thrilling exploration of Artificial Intelligence (AI) and its gifted progeny, ChatGPT-4. Picture AI as a once-imagined creature from a fairy tale, now alive and thriving in our everyday reality, shaping the course of our lives and our businesses. As we lay the groundwork of understanding AI, it's akin to learning the alphabet before penning a novel. We're not merely understanding AI, we're grasping how to wield it as a powerful tool for business marketing. As we delve into the repertoire of ChatGPT-4, a remarkable offspring of AI, we'll learn how it can spin webs of engaging content, gracefully manage the dance of social media, and compose symphonies of effective email marketing.

A Brief History of AI: From Fantasy to Reality

Let's take a trip back in time. Not too far back, just a few decades. Picture a world without smartphones, without the internet, without the comfort of asking Siri to set a reminder or Alexa to play your favorite song. In this world, the idea of a machine that could think like a human was just that - an idea, a fantasy. This was the starting point of our journey into the realm of Artificial Intelligence (AI). Buckle up, folks, it's going to be a wild ride!

Our story begins in the 1950s, with a bunch of enthusiastic scientists who sounded more like science fiction writers. They proposed a revolutionary idea: Could machines be made to simulate human intelligence? This was the birth of AI, and the beginning of our journey.

Jump forward to the 1960s and '70s, and AI was like a toddler, taking its first steps. We saw the creation of ELIZA and SHRDLU, early programs that could understand and respond to natural language. But let's be honest, these were more of a one-trick pony. They could do some tasks impressively, but they were far from the versatile AI we dreamt of.

Then came the 'AI Winter' of the 1980s. Funding was cut, interest waned, and AI was like a teen going through a phase. It was all doom and gloom. But, like every good story, there was a twist. Researchers were quietly developing new methods and technologies, laying the groundwork for the AI renaissance that was to come.

The 1990s and early 2000s saw the rise of Machine Learning. Now, this is where things start to get exciting. AI was no longer just programmed to perform tasks, it was learning to do them on its own! It was like the difference between learning to parrot a phrase in a foreign language and actually understanding the language.

Fast forward to the 2010s, and we entered the era of Deep Learning. AI was now capable of interpreting complex patterns and making decisions, mimicking the human brain's own process. This was the game-changer, the moment AI went from being a useful tool to a potential revolution.

And here we are now, in the era of AI ubiquity. From our smartphones to our cars, AI is everywhere. And with the rise of AI models like GPT-3 and GPT-4, we're inching closer to the original dream of machines that can truly simulate human intelligence.

In summary,

1. **The Birth of AI (1950s):** AI was born from the idea of creating machines that could simulate human intelligence.

2. **Early Developments (1960s and '70s):** Early AI programs like ELIZA and SHRDLU demonstrated the potential of machines to understand and respond to natural language.

3. **The AI Winter (1980s):** A period of decreased interest and funding in AI research, but with important groundwork being laid behind the scenes.

4. **The Rise of Machine Learning (1990s to early 2000s):** A shift towards AI that could learn to perform tasks on its own, rather than just being programmed.

5. **The Era of Deep Learning (2010s):** AI became capable of interpreting complex patterns and making decisions, a game-changing development.

6. **AI Today: Ubiquity and Future Prospects:** AI is everywhere in our lives today, and with developments like GPT-3 and GPT-4, we're closer than ever to realizing the dream of machines that can truly simulate human intelligence.

From GPT-3 to GPT-4: Key Updates and Improvements

Imagine for a moment, you're at a car dealership. You've been happily driving a trusty GPT-3 model for a while. It's a solid machine, gets you from A to B with minimal fuss, and has some pretty cool features. But then, the salesman shows you the new GPT-4 model. It's sleek, it's powerful, and it's full of upgrades that make your GPT-3 look like a horse and cart. That, my friends, is the leap from GPT-3 to GPT-4.

The first major update? GPT-4 has learned to see! Not in the literal sense of course, but it can now handle multiple types of input, not just text. You can feed it images and it'll generate descriptions, captions, or even whole stories based on the visuals. It's like going from reading a book to watching a movie - a whole new way to experience the world!

Next up, we've got the ability to understand and generate content in multiple languages. GPT-4 is your new multilingual best friend. It's like having a personal translator who not only speaks 60 languages but also understands cultural nuances and colloquialisms.

And finally, the cherry on top: performance. GPT-4 is not just bigger, but it's also better. It responds faster, understands deeper, and is more accurate than ever. Remember the old days when you asked Siri a question and she would respond with something utterly unrelated? Well, those days are over. GPT-4 is like having a top student in your pocket, ready to help you ace any exam.

Wrapping this section up, remember

1. **Multi-Modal Inputs:** GPT-4 can handle multiple types of input, including images. It's like adding eyes to your AI, providing a richer and more immersive experience.

2. **Multilingual Capabilities:** GPT-4 can understand and generate content in multiple languages, making it the perfect global companion.

3. **Improved Performance:** GPT-4 is faster, more accurate, and deeper in understanding. It's like upgrading from a reliable sedan to a high-performance sports car.

4. **Evolution of AI:** The jump from GPT-3 to GPT-4 is a testament to the rapid progress in AI technology, giving us a glimpse into the exciting future that lies ahead.

With these upgrades, GPT-4 is not just a new model. It's a game changer, setting a new standard for what AI can do.

Understanding Natural Language Processing

Ever had a moment when you've uttered something and the other person completely misinterpreted it? It's frustrating, isn't it? Now, imagine teaching a computer to understand not just words, but the meaning behind them. Welcome to the world of Natural Language Processing or NLP as the tech folks like to call it.

In essence, NLP is a bit like a translator between humans and computers. It's how your laptop or phone understands your typed or spoken words. But here's the twist: language isn't just about words. It's about context, tone, even sarcasm. And that's where NLP really shines.

Remember when you used to diagram sentences in English class? Subject, verb, object, and so on? That's the basic idea behind 'syntax,' one of the key components of NLP. It's all about how words in a sentence fit together. It's the jigsaw puzzle of language.

But what about the meaning of the words? That's where 'semantics' come in. Semantics deal with the meaning of words and how they convey an idea or concept. It's like the color palette of language, giving hues and shades to the black and white sketch that syntax provides.

And finally, we have 'pragmatics.' Now, this is the real deal. It's about understanding language in context. It's what enables a computer to tell the difference between "I'm fine" when you've just won the lottery, and "I'm fine" when you've just stubbed your toe on a door. It's the fine wine of language - nuanced and rich.

So next time when you say "Hey Siri" or "Okay Google" and it actually understands you, remember you've got NLP to thank for it. It's the quiet hero behind the scenes, making our tech savvy world a little more human.

Some key points:

1. **Natural Language Processing (NLP):** This technology allows computers to understand and interpret human language. It's the bridge between human communication and machine understanding.

2. **Syntax:** The structure of sentences. It's the building blocks, the jigsaw puzzle of language.

3. **Semantics:** The meaning of words and sentences. It's the color palette, adding vibrancy and depth to language.

4. **Pragmatics:** Understanding language in context. It's the fine wine of language, adding nuance and richness.

5. **NLP in Daily Life:** Every time you use voice commands or type a search query, you're benefiting from NLP. It's the unsung hero making technology more human-friendly.

Chapter 2:
ChatGPT-4: A Revolutionary AI Tool

In Chapter 2, we dive into the ocean of ChatGPT-4, a revolutionary creation in AI that stands poised to reshape the landscapes of business operations. Picture us illustrating a vivid panorama of ChatGPT-4, detailing its unique characteristics and remarkable abilities. Our quest is to guide you in harnessing ChatGPT-4 for your enterprise, so you can begin to experience the richness of its offerings. Whether your aim is to enhance content creation, elevate customer service, or transform your overall marketing strategy, ChatGPT-4 stands as a reliable ally in achieving your objectives.

Overview of ChatGPT-4

Imagine, if you will, a world where your computer understands you better than your best friend. Not only your words but the images you show it, too. Welcome to the world of ChatGPT-4, the supercharged upgrade of artificial intelligence that's making this reality come alive.

First, let's get to know an impressive feature of GPT-4, the 'multimodal input.' Now, before you get lost in jargon-land, let me explain. 'Multimodal input' simply means GPT-4 can comprehend both text and images. Think of it as a well-read art connoisseur – it knows its Shakespeare as well as its Picasso.

Next up, we have language proficiency. GPT-4 is like that one friend who speaks a dozen languages. Whether you say "Hello," "Hola," or "Bonjour," GPT-4 can reply, making it a perfect partner for those late-night language practice sessions.

But the improvements don't stop there. GPT-4 isn't just about understanding better; it's about responding better, too. It crafts responses with such accuracy and context-awareness that you'd think you're in a conversation with a human. It's like having a chat with the most engaging person at the party, minus any awkward small talk.

And now, for the grand finale. GPT-4 can browse the web in real-time. Yes, you heard it right. This AI can fetch information from the internet faster than your nephew can beat you at a video game. From sports scores to trivia about Bhutan's capital, GPT-4 is your personal trivia champion.

In a nutshell, GPT-4 is not just an AI. It's a multilingual, art-loving, internet-surfing, conversation wizard. It's here to redefine how you interact with technology.

Key points to remember:

1. **Multimodal Capabilities:** GPT-4 can understand and interpret both text and images.

2. **Language Proficiency:** GPT-4 is multilingual, making it a valuable asset in our globalized world.

3. **Enhanced Responses:** GPT-4 generates precise and context-aware responses, enhancing the quality of interactions.

4. **Internet Browsing:** GPT-4 can access and retrieve information from the web in real-time.

5. **GPT-4 Redefines Interactions:** With these features, GPT-4 is revolutionizing how we interact with technology.

Key Features and Capabilities

Prepare to have your minds blown as we dive deep into the mesmerizing world of its key features and capabilities. This extraordinary AI tool is like a magic show for your business, enchanting your audience and igniting your marketing strategies with a touch of genius. Picture it as a master illusionist, seamlessly blending cutting-edge technology with the art of captivating conversation. So, gather 'round as we unveil the secrets behind ChatGPT-4's mind-boggling abilities and unlock the door to business success like never before.

1. **Conversational Brilliance:** ChatGPT-4 possesses a gift for conversation that would make even the most seasoned talk show host envious. It navigates the twists and turns of dialogue effortlessly, providing engaging and contextually relevant responses. This ability to communicate in a natural and authentic manner is what sets ChatGPT-4 apart, making it an indispensable asset for businesses aiming to connect with their customers on a deeper level.

2. **Adaptive Learning:** Like a shapeshifter in the realm of AI, ChatGPT-4 has the uncanny ability to adapt and evolve. It learns from each interaction, refining its understanding of human language, preferences, and nuances. This adaptive learning enables ChatGPT-4 to continuously improve its responses, ensuring that every conversation is more effective than the last. Prepare to be amazed as you witness ChatGPT-4 grow and tailor its capabilities to suit your specific business needs.

3. **Multimodal Mastery:** Visuals speak volumes, and ChatGPT-4 understands this profoundly. It possesses

the extraordinary capability to interpret both text and images, unleashing a world of possibilities. Imagine engaging your audience with captivating visuals while ChatGPT-4 supplements your content with intelligent insights and compelling narratives. Together, you create a symphony of text and visuals that resonates deeply with your target audience.

4. **Vast Knowledge Repository:** ChatGPT-4 is an intellectual powerhouse, armed with a vast repository of knowledge. It effortlessly retrieves information on a wide range of topics, providing accurate and reliable answers to your questions. Say goodbye to frantic web searches and welcome the convenience of having an AI companion well-versed in a multitude of subjects at your disposal.

5. **Cross-Language Competence:** The language barrier is no longer a hindrance to global business endeavors. ChatGPT-4 stands tall as a multilingual marvel, capable of understanding and responding in multiple languages. Whether you're engaging with international clients, expanding into new markets, or collaborating with global teams, ChatGPT-4 serves as your trusted language bridge, fostering communication and driving success.

6. **Real-Time Support:** Picture having a 24/7 AI assistant by your side, ready to lend a helping hand whenever you need it. ChatGPT-4 provides real-time support, ensuring that assistance is just a conversation away. Whether it's resolving customer queries, guiding users through complex processes, or offering personalized recommendations, ChatGPT-4 is your tireless ally in delivering exceptional customer experiences.

7. **Privacy and Security:** Trust is the foundation of any successful relationship. With ChatGPT-4, you can rest assured that your data is treated with utmost care and confidentiality. Robust privacy measures are in place to safeguard your information, providing you with peace of mind as you explore the boundless possibilities of this AI tool.

8. **User-Friendly Interface:** You don't need to be a tech whiz to unlock the power of ChatGPT-4. Its user-friendly interface ensures a seamless and intuitive experience for users of all backgrounds. The focus is on simplicity and accessibility, allowing you to harness the full potential of this AI tool without the need for extensive technical knowledge.

9. **Ongoing Advancements:** The world of AI is a rapidly evolving landscape, and ChatGPT-4 is no exception. The dedicated team behind its development is committed to continuous advancements and updates. You can expect regular enhancements and new features that keep pace with the ever-changing business environment, empowering you to stay ahead of the competition.

10. **Integration Flexibility:** ChatGPT-4 seamlessly integrates with existing tools and platforms, making it a versatile addition to your business ecosystem. Whether it's integrating with your website, social media platforms, or customer support systems, ChatGPT-4 effortlessly adapts to your infrastructure, amplifying its capabilities across various channels.

With these key features and capabilities of ChatGPT-4 at your fingertips, you're now equipped to unlock its full potential in revolutionizing your business marketing strategies.

Setting up ChatGPT-4 for Your Business

As we dance into the next chapter of our AI symphony, we turn our attention to the practicalities of integrating ChatGPT-4 into your business marketing strategy. Imagine you're setting up a new instrument in your orchestra - you wouldn't just place it randomly, right? You'd need to tune it, position it correctly, and ensure it harmonizes with the rest of the ensemble. That's what we're going to do with ChatGPT-4.

The first step is akin to finding the right spot for our instrument. You need to define the role of ChatGPT-4 in your business. Do you want it to generate leads, improve customer service, or perhaps provide product recommendations? The role you define will guide the setup process and determine how ChatGPT-4 interacts with your customers.

Next, you need to configure ChatGPT-4 to fit your specific needs, much like tuning an instrument. You can adjust the settings to ensure it matches your brand voice, uses the right language and tone, and provides accurate and helpful responses. ChatGPT-4 comes with a plethora of customization options, allowing you to craft a unique AI experience that aligns with your brand identity.

The last step is to integrate ChatGPT-4 into your existing systems. This is akin to ensuring our new instrument can play in harmony with the rest of the orchestra. Depending on your business, this might involve integrating ChatGPT-4 with your website, your social media platforms, your customer relationship management system, or any other platforms where you interact with customers. The goal is to create a seamless experience where ChatGPT-4 becomes a natural extension of your brand.

Let's recap the key points:

1. Define the role of ChatGPT-4 in your business.

2. Configure ChatGPT-4 to match your brand voice and customer needs.

3. Integrate ChatGPT-4 into your existing systems to create a seamless customer experience.

In the next section, we'll dive deeper into the art of optimizing ChatGPT-4 for your business. We'll explore how to maximize the effectiveness of this new member of your marketing orchestra, and share practical tips for fine-tuning ChatGPT-4 to achieve real, measurable results. As with any instrument, the true magic happens when it's played well. Let's turn this technology into beautiful music for your business.

PART II:
ChatGPT-4 for Business Marketing

Chapter 3:
Harnessing the Power of ChatGPT-4 for Your Business

Chapter 3 unveils the enchanting prospects of utilizing ChatGPT-4 for the art of content creation and blogging. As we journey further into the AI wilderness, we'll examine the facets and functions of ChatGPT-4 that make it an exceptional tool for content crafting. From concocting blog entries to fashioning social media content, ChatGPT-4 assists businesses in refining their content creation process, producing quality material that strikes a chord with their intended audience.

ChatGPT-4 for Content Creation and Blogging

As we continue our exploration of AI in marketing, it's time to pull back the curtain on one of the most exciting applications of ChatGPT-4: content creation and blogging. Picture this: you're in a band and you need to write a new song. You have the melody, but you're stuck on the lyrics. Wouldn't it be great if you could turn to a band member and say, "Hey, can you help me finish this verse?" That's what ChatGPT-4 can do for your content creation process.

Just as a seasoned songwriter can take a melody and craft fitting lyrics, ChatGPT-4 can take your ideas and craft engaging, relevant content. You provide the topic, the tone, and any specific details you want included, and ChatGPT-4 does the rest. It's like having a personal copywriter who's available 24/7, never gets writer's block, and can generate blog posts, articles, and social media updates at lightning speed.

Of course, it's not just about speed. ChatGPT-4 is trained on a vast range of data, which means it can generate content on a wide variety of topics. Whether you're writing a technical piece about your latest product, a thought leadership article on industry trends, or an engaging blog post for your customers, ChatGPT-4 can help.

The key is to guide ChatGPT-4, like a band leader conducting the orchestra. Set the stage with your initial instructions, then fine-tune the output until it hits all the right notes. And remember, while ChatGPT-4 can generate the bulk of your content, a human touch can add that spark of authenticity that resonates with readers.

To summarize:

1. ChatGPT-4 can act as a personal copywriter, generating content at high speed.

2. It can write on a wide variety of topics, making it a versatile tool in your content creation toolbox.

3. Guiding and fine-tuning the output of ChatGPT-4 can help ensure the content aligns with your brand and resonates with your audience.

In the next chapter, we'll put ChatGPT-4 to work in another key area of business marketing: email marketing and newsletters. We'll explore how to use ChatGPT-4 to craft engaging emails, personalize content for different segments of your audience, and automate your email marketing process. Stay tuned, because this will be like adding a virtuoso soloist to your marketing orchestra.

Using ChatGPT-4 for Email Marketing and Newsletters

We have now entered the vast landscape of Email Marketing and Newsletters, an arena where ChatGPT-4 can perform remarkable feats. Email marketing is like throwing a message in a bottle into the vast ocean of the internet, hoping it will wash ashore at the right person's inbox. Your message must be compelling, personalized, and valuable to catch your recipient's eye amidst the daily flood of emails. Here, the abilities of ChatGPT-4 to process large amounts of data and generate human-like text come into play.

When we say ChatGPT-4 can help with email marketing, it's not just about using it to write attractive email subject lines, although it's pretty good at that too. It's about how it can help you craft individualized emails at scale. Picture this – you're a small business owner with a clientele of a thousand. Imagine having to draft a unique and engaging email for each customer. Daunting, isn't it? ChatGPT-4 can take your customer data, understand their preferences and interactions with your business, and create personalized emails for each one. It's like having an army of copywriters at your disposal.

Newsletters are another area where ChatGPT-4 shines. Regularly updating your audience with engaging content can be a challenge. ChatGPT-4 can generate a stream of fresh content, ensuring your newsletter always provides value and maintains the interest of your subscribers. Whether it's writing summaries of recent blog posts, sharing company updates, or providing industry insights, ChatGPT-4 has got you covered.

So how does one go about integrating ChatGPT-4 into their email marketing strategy? The first step is to understand your audience. You need to feed ChatGPT-4 relevant data so it can generate personalized content. This could be customer purchase history, interactions with previous emails, or general demographic information. Next, you must define the purpose of your email. Are you looking to promote a new product, share news, or maybe re-engage dormant customers? Once you know your goal, you can instruct ChatGPT-4 to generate content that aligns with it.

Remember, while ChatGPT-4 can generate content, it's up to you to add the human touch. Review the content generated by ChatGPT-4, tweak it if necessary, and ensure it aligns with your brand voice. Think of ChatGPT-4 as a tool, not a replacement for human creativity. The most successful email marketing campaigns are a blend of artificial intelligence and human intuition.

Also, it's crucial to remember the legal and ethical implications of email marketing. Ensure you are complying with all regulations and respecting the privacy of your customers. Just because you can personalize emails with ChatGPT-4 doesn't mean you should use all the data at your disposal. Be mindful of your customers' boundaries.

In conclusion, using ChatGPT-4 for email marketing and newsletters can be a game-changer. It can help you personalize your emails, generate engaging content for your newsletters, and save you time and effort. However, remember to use it responsibly and always add your unique human touch to the mix.

Key points:

1. ChatGPT-4 can help you generate personalized emails and engaging newsletters.

2. Understand your audience and define your email's purpose before using ChatGPT-4.

3. Review and tweak the content generated by ChatGPT-4 to ensure it aligns with your brand voice.

4. Be mindful of the legal and ethical implications of email marketing.

As we move forward, let's dive into the realm of customer service. We'll explore how ChatGPT-4 can transform your customer interactions, creating experiences that not only satisfy but delight. Let's unveil the potential of "ChatGPT-4 for Customer Service: Chatbots and More".

ChatGPT-4 for Customer Service: Chatbots and More

From the transformative vistas of the previous section, we now edge towards a realm where technology and customer service intersect, creating a powerful symbiotic relationship that businesses can leverage to great effect. Enter ChatGPT-4, an artificial intelligence tool that has revolutionized the customer service industry, reshaping it into an arena where customers interact with sophisticated chatbots that deliver personalized, real-time assistance with the accuracy of a trained human agent.

At the heart of ChatGPT-4 is a concept known as machine learning, a form of artificial intelligence that allows computers to learn from their experiences without being explicitly programmed. In simpler terms, imagine teaching a child to recognize a cat. You show them pictures of cats, and after a while, they can identify a cat even if they've never seen that particular cat before. That's essentially what machine learning does, but with immense quantities of data.

Chatbots, the primary agents of interaction in this AI-driven customer service landscape, are digital entities designed to simulate human conversation. They're like your friendly neighborhood shopkeeper, always ready to assist, but in this case, they never sleep or take a break. The unique aspect about ChatGPT-4 powered chatbots is their ability to understand context, maintain a conversation thread, and even exhibit a level of empathy, making them not just response machines, but rather, conversation partners.

These chatbots do more than just answer customer inquiries. They are a dynamic force that can perform a myriad of tasks, from scheduling appointments to suggesting products based on customer preferences, acting as a virtual assistant that is available around the clock. The potential applications are vast and can be tailored to fit any business, large or small.

Now, imagine this: A customer has a question about your product at 2:00 AM. Instead of waiting for office hours, they interact with a chatbot that resolves their query on the spot. This immediate and efficient service enhances customer satisfaction and fosters a sense of loyalty towards your brand, which in turn, drives repeat business. It's like having a fleet of customer service representatives, ever-ready, without the cost and logistical challenges of managing a human workforce.

But the magic of ChatGPT-4 doesn't stop at chatbots. This technology can also be integrated into email marketing, social media responses, and even phone systems, offering a seamless, unified customer service experience that can adapt to the preferences of each individual customer. The possibilities are as broad as your imagination, waiting to be explored and harnessed for the success of your business.

In the end, the adoption of ChatGPT-4 in customer service isn't just about streamlining processes or cutting costs. It's about crafting unique, personalized experiences for your customers, making them feel valued and heard. It's about standing out in the crowd and creating a memorable brand that customers can trust and rely on.

To encapsulate, let's summarize the key points:

1. ChatGPT-4 is an advanced AI tool that uses machine learning to provide highly effective, personalized customer service through chatbots and other platforms.

2. Chatbots are digital entities that simulate human conversation, able to assist customers in real-time, 24/7, performing tasks from answering inquiries to scheduling appointments.

3. The integration of ChatGPT-4 in customer service can lead to increased customer satisfaction, brand loyalty, and repeat business.

4. The technology can be utilized in various customer service channels, including email marketing, social media, and phone systems, offering a unified customer service experience.

5. The ultimate goal of ChatGPT-4 adoption is to create personalized experiences for customers, making them feel valued, and building a memorable, trustworthy brand.

In the next chapter, we will delve deeper into how businesses can best implement this transformative technology. So, stay tuned as we continue our journey, exploring the intricacies of AI and the myriad ways it can help your business thrive in the digital age.

Chapter 4:
ChatGPT-4 for Social Media Marketing

In this chapter, we explore the ways in which businesses can leverage the power of AI to create engaging social media content. Social media platforms like Facebook, Twitter, and Instagram have become essential marketing channels for businesses of all sizes. By using ChatGPT-4, businesses can generate high-quality content that resonates with their target audience. ChatGPT-4 can analyze customer feedback and generate personalized content that speaks directly to the needs and interests of individual customers. However, it's important to note that social media marketing is a constantly evolving field, and businesses must stay up-to-date on the latest trends and best practices to succeed. By using ChatGPT-4 in conjunction with other social media marketing tools and techniques, businesses can create a powerful and effective social media strategy that drives real results.

Creating Engaging Social Media Posts with CHAT GPT-4

In the shimmering landscape of the digital age, social media has emerged as the town square, a bustling meeting place where brands and consumers interact, share ideas, and forge meaningful connections. The spotlight now swings towards ChatGPT-4's ability to elevate your brand's social media presence, painting it with shades of creativity, relevance, and engagement that resonates with your audience.

Social media marketing, to put it simply, is the use of social media platforms to connect with your audience, build your brand, increase sales, and drive website traffic. It involves publishing great content, listening to and engaging your followers, analyzing your results, and running social media advertisements.

ChatGPT-4, with its advanced natural language processing capabilities, is like an artist's palette, brimming with colors waiting to be mixed and matched to create captivating social media content. Natural language processing, or NLP, is a field of artificial intelligence that focuses on the interaction between humans and computers using natural language. The ultimate objective of NLP is to read, decipher, understand, and make sense of the human language in a valuable way. In simpler terms, it's like teaching a computer to understand and speak human language.

Imagine being able to create posts that resonate with your audience's current mood, cultural events, or trending topics, all with a few commands to ChatGPT-4. It's akin to having a seasoned copywriter, social media manager, and trend analyst rolled into one, working tirelessly to keep your brand at the forefront of social media engagement.

But it's not just about creating engaging posts. ChatGPT-4 can also help analyze responses, gather insights, and tweak strategies based on the feedback received. It's like having an ongoing conversation with your audience, constantly learning, adapting, and serving them better.

Let's say you're a small business owner who sells handmade candles. You can use ChatGPT-4 to create posts showcasing your products, share stories behind the creation of each candle, suggest gifting ideas, and even answer customer queries in the comments section. This way, you not only promote your products but also build a community that appreciates your craft and supports your business.

Harnessing ChatGPT-4 for your social media marketing efforts can result in a more engaging, dynamic, and personalized brand presence. It's about creating a connection that goes beyond a simple follow or like, turning your followers into fans, customers, and even brand ambassadors.

To summarize this section, here are the key takeaways:

1. Social media marketing is a powerful tool for businesses to connect with their audience, build their brand, increase sales, and drive website traffic.

2. ChatGPT-4, with its natural language processing capabilities, can help create engaging and relevant social media content that resonates with your audience.

3. Beyond creating posts, ChatGPT-4 can analyze responses, gather insights, and adapt strategies to better serve your audience.

4. By creating a dynamic and personalized social media presence, businesses can turn followers into fans, customers, and brand ambassadors.

Automating Social Media Management with ChatGPT-4

As we continue our exploration, we take a step beyond simply creating engaging social media content to delve into how ChatGPT-4 can serve as a comprehensive conductor for your social media orchestra. This section takes us into the realm of social media management automation, where ChatGPT-4 plays a pivotal role in orchestrating your brand's social media activities.

Social media management entails overseeing your online interactions and content across various social media platforms like Facebook, Instagram, Twitter, and Pinterest. It goes beyond just posting updates to your company's social media profiles. It also includes engaging with your audience and looking for new opportunities to increase reach and visibility.

In the digital world, time is a commodity more precious than gold. Automation, in essence, is the technique of making a process or system operate automatically, thereby saving time and resources. Imagine being able to schedule posts, respond to comments, track mentions of your brand, and analyze performance metrics, all while you focus on other aspects of your business. That's the power of automating social media management with ChatGPT-4.

ChatGPT-4 can be your own personal social media manager, a tireless entity that keeps your social media presence vibrant, relevant, and engaging. It can schedule posts at optimal times for maximum engagement, respond to comments and messages in real-time, track mentions of your brand and related keywords, and provide insights on your social media performance.

Consider the power of sentiment analysis, an aspect of ChatGPT-4's machine learning capabilities, which allows it to understand the tone of comments and messages, distinguishing between positive, neutral, and negative sentiments. This allows you to address customer concerns promptly and celebrate positive feedback, thereby enhancing your brand image and customer satisfaction.

Moreover, ChatGPT-4 can also keep a finger on the pulse of current trends and popular hashtags, helping your brand stay relevant and participate in ongoing conversations. In a way, it's like having a dedicated researcher constantly providing fresh, relevant information.

In sum, automating your social media management with ChatGPT-4 not only increases efficiency and saves time but also ensures a consistent, engaging, and responsive brand presence across various social media platforms.

Let's encapsulate the key points:

1. Social media management involves overseeing your brand's online interactions and content across various social media platforms.

2. Automating social media management with ChatGPT-4 can save time and resources, allowing you to focus on other aspects of your business.

3. ChatGPT-4 can schedule posts, respond to comments and messages, track brand mentions, and provide performance insights.

4. Through sentiment analysis, ChatGPT-4 can understand and categorize the tone of comments and messages, allowing prompt response to customer feedback.

5. ChatGPT-4 can help your brand stay relevant by keeping track of current trends and popular hashtags.

Case Studies: Successful Social Media Campaigns with ChatGPT-4

As we transition from the previous section, let's delve into a fascinating realm where theory meets practice. To truly appreciate the transformative power of ChatGPT-4 in the world of social media, we turn our gaze to a collection of real-world stories. Here, success isn't just an aspiration, but a reality made possible by the smart application of AI.

Examples are from the research site https://research.aimultiple.com.

Our first stop is HelloFresh Freddy, a customer service chatbot launched by HelloFresh. This chatbot, though modest in its conversational abilities, significantly improved user engagement and satisfaction. HelloFresh Freddy managed surveys and quizzes, sent automated deals to users who correctly responded to quizzes, and even suggested recipes. The result was a 76% reduction in response time and a 47% boost in incoming messages. Just imagine, a digital assistant that can not only guide your customer's journey but also make it more engaging and efficient!

Next, we move on to the healthcare sector, where chatbots have been making waves. During the Covid-19 outbreak, the government of India collaborated with Haptik to develop a WhatsApp chatbot to counteract misinformation, address people's questions, and educate them swiftly. The chatbot, built in just five days, was able to respond in both Hindi and English. In a world where misinformation can spread as fast as a virus, having an AI-powered ally can be a game-changer.

The healthcare app HealthTap developed Dr. A.I., a chatbot that reads patients' symptoms, asks follow-up questions, and connects patients with a specialized doctor nearby. Not just a middleman, Dr. A.I. also gives recommendations on what steps the patient should take next. Similarly, Melody, an AI developed by Baidu, China's equivalent to Google, collects symptoms from patients and summarizes them for doctors, potentially saving lives in times of health worker shortages.

Let's not forget the mental health sector. Woebot, a free therapy chatbot, uses cognitive-behavioral therapy to deliver scripted responses to users. The chatbot has shown significant benefits for college students dealing with depression. Similarly, Wysa, a therapy chatbot, helps individuals navigate through stress, depression, anxiety, and other psychological distresses, and has received positive reviews from its users.

Snapchat's My AI chatbot, utilizing Open AI's GPT technology, is an excellent example of how AI chatbots are becoming mainstream in social media platforms. The chatbot can send AI-generated images and show "sponsored links" based on the user's conversation topics, enhancing the user experience while also opening up new avenues for targeted marketing.

In sum, the key points we've discovered from these case studies are:

1. ChatGPT-4 can significantly reduce response times and increase user engagement, as seen with HelloFresh Freddy.

2. In times of crisis, such as during the Covid-19 pandemic, chatbots can provide timely and accurate information to large populations.

3. Chatbots like Dr. A.I. and Melody are revolutionizing the healthcare sector by helping patients connect with the right specialists and summarizing symptoms for doctors.

4. Therapeutic chatbots like Woebot and Wysa are providing mental health support to those who need it.

5. On social media platforms, chatbots are enhancing user experience by providing personalized content and sponsored links based on the user's interests.

Now, with a rich understanding of how ChatGPT-4 has been used in successful social media campaigns, let's turn our gaze to the future. As we move on to the next chapter, we'll explore another dynamic platform for marketing: YouTube. "Leveraging ChatGPT-4 for YouTube and Video Marketing" will open up a new world of possibilities, showing you how AI can bring video content to life like never before.

Chapter 5:
Leveraging ChatGPT-4 for YouTube and Video Marketing

This chapter explores the ways in which businesses can use AI to create compelling video content that resonates with their target audience. Video marketing has become an increasingly important part of the marketing mix, with platforms like YouTube and TikTok providing new opportunities for businesses to connect with customers. By using ChatGPT-4, businesses can generate high-quality video scripts that capture the attention of viewers and drive engagement. ChatGPT-4 can analyze customer feedback and generate personalized video content that speaks directly to the needs and interests of individual customers. However, it's important to note that video marketing is a complex and competitive field, and businesses must stay up-to-date on the latest trends and best practices to succeed. By using ChatGPT-4 in conjunction with other video marketing tools and techniques, businesses can create a powerful and effective video marketing strategy that drives real results.

Script Writing with ChatGPT-4

As we journey further into the fascinating realm of artificial intelligence, we'll now turn our attention to script writing with ChatGPT-4, a transformative tool that's reshaping the landscape of content creation.

Script writing, at its core, is about weaving together compelling narratives that captivate audiences, drawing them into an immersive world of dialogue and action. Yet, for many, the task of drafting a captivating script can be daunting, fraught with writer's block and long hours. Enter

ChatGPT-4, an AI model adept at generating human-like text. With this tool at your fingertips, the scriptwriting process becomes not only simpler but also more dynamic and innovative.

So, how does it work? ChatGPT-4, the fourth iteration of the Generative Pretrained Transformer models developed by OpenAI, leverages the power of machine learning. It's trained on a vast array of internet text, and as such, it learns patterns, contexts, and the nuances of human language. Once trained, it can generate text that mirrors the style and tone of the input it's given. Therefore, when you provide ChatGPT-4 with a prompt for your script, such as a line of dialogue or a narrative scenario, the model can build upon it to create a rich, engaging script.

Yet, the real magic of using ChatGPT-4 in scriptwriting lies not merely in its ability to generate text, but in its capacity to serve as a springboard for creativity. It's akin to having a collaborative writing partner, one that offers ideas and phrases that can spark your imagination, pushing your script into unexpected and exciting directions.

However, it's critical to approach this tool with an understanding of its limitations. AI, as advanced as it is, doesn't possess human intuition or emotional intelligence. While ChatGPT-4 can provide the skeleton of your script, it's up to you, the human writer, to breathe life into it with your unique perspective and emotional depth.

Now, let's distill these insights into key points:

1. ChatGPT-4 is an AI model capable of generating human-like text, making it a valuable tool for scriptwriting.

2. The model generates text based on the input it receives, allowing you to guide its tone and style.

3. ChatGPT-4 can serve as a source of inspiration, offering ideas that can steer your script in novel directions.

4. While powerful, ChatGPT-4 doesn't possess human intuition or emotional intelligence, necessitating the human writer's touch to fully realize a script's potential.

As we close this section, we find ourselves at the precipice of another AI-enhanced frontier: Video Descriptions and SEO with ChatGPT-4. In this upcoming section, we'll explore how the power of AI can be harnessed to optimize video content for search engines, opening up a world of possibilities for visibility and reach. Let's continue our journey.

Video Descriptions and SEO with ChatGPT-4

Continuing our journey into the dynamic world of artificial intelligence, we now venture into the realm of video descriptions and Search Engine Optimization (SEO) with ChatGPT-4. Let's unpack this concept to understand how it can supercharge your video marketing strategy.

Imagine you're a filmmaker who just crafted a captivating video. Now, the challenge lies in ensuring that your masterpiece reaches the widest audience possible. This is where the power of video descriptions and SEO come into play. SEO, or Search Engine Optimization, is the practice of enhancing your online content so that a search engine, like Google or YouTube, will show it as a top result for searches of certain keywords. Video descriptions are crucial in this process, serving as a written summary that search engines can 'read' to understand the content of your video.

Now, you might ask, how does ChatGPT-4 fit into this picture? Well, ChatGPT-4, with its proficiency in generating engaging, human-like text, can be employed to craft compelling video descriptions that are also SEO-optimized. It can understand the context of your video, generate a description that accurately reflects its content, and weave in relevant keywords that can help your video surface in search results. It's like having a skilled copywriter and SEO expert combined into one!

However, let's remember to take this tool with a grain of salt. While ChatGPT-4 can generate descriptions and suggest keywords, the final decision still lies in your hands. It's critical to review and tweak the AI's output to ensure it aligns with your video content and audience expectations.

Let's distill the key points of this section:

1. Video descriptions and SEO are pivotal in improving the visibility of your video content on search engines.

2. ChatGPT-4 can assist in crafting compelling, SEO-optimized video descriptions by generating engaging, human-like text.

3. The AI model can understand the context of your video and suggest relevant keywords, enhancing the SEO potential of your content.

4. Despite its capabilities, ChatGPT-4's output should be reviewed and adjusted by a human to ensure alignment with video content and audience expectations.

As we conclude this enlightening exploration of video descriptions and SEO with ChatGPT-4, we look forward to our next destination - growing your YouTube presence with ChatGPT-4. In the following section, we'll delve into how this powerful AI can be a game-changer in expanding your reach and engagement on YouTube, the world's largest video sharing platform.

Growing Your YouTube Presence with ChatGPT-4

With a strong grasp on video descriptions and SEO with ChatGPT-4, let's now turn our attention to a new frontier: Growing your YouTube presence with ChatGPT-4. As we embark on this journey, keep in mind that YouTube is more than just a video hosting site; it's a vibrant community where ideas are shared, stories are told, and businesses are built.

Now, where does ChatGPT-4 come into the picture? Imagine having a digital assistant that can not only help you manage your YouTube channel but also provide you with insights and strategies to grow your audience. That's what ChatGPT-4 can do. It can help you identify trends, understand your audience, and craft content that resonates with them.

One of the ways ChatGPT-4 can assist you is by analyzing your YouTube comments. It can sift through the sea of feedback, identify common themes, and provide you with a distilled view of what your viewers like and don't like. With this information, you can adjust your content strategy to better meet your audience's preferences.

Additionally, ChatGPT-4 can aid in scriptwriting for your YouTube videos. We've already discussed how this AI can help with scriptwriting, but let's not forget its application here. A well-written script can engage your audience, keep them watching, and encourage them to interact with your content, thereby boosting your YouTube presence.

Let's not forget the importance of consistent interaction with your audience. With ChatGPT-4, you can automate responses to comments, ensuring that your audience feels heard and valued. The AI can craft personalized responses that can foster a sense of community and encourage viewers to engage more with your content.

Here's a recap of the key points from this section:

1. ChatGPT-4 can help grow your YouTube presence by providing insights into your audience's preferences, assisting in scriptwriting, and automating responses to comments.

2. The AI can analyze your YouTube comments to understand what your viewers like and dislike, enabling you to adjust your content strategy accordingly.

3. ChatGPT-4 can assist in scriptwriting for YouTube videos, helping to create engaging content that keeps viewers watching and interacting.

4. By automating responses to comments, ChatGPT-4 can foster a sense of community on your YouTube channel, encouraging more viewer engagement.

As we conclude this section on growing your YouTube presence with ChatGPT-4, it's time to raise the stakes. As we transition into "PART III: Advanced Techniques and Strategies," we'll delve deeper into the power of ChatGPT-4 and explore how it can be leveraged to its fullest potential. The journey has been exciting so far, and the best is yet to come.

PART III:
Advanced Techniques and Strategies

Chapter 6:
Mastering ChatGPT-4 for Lead Generation

Chapter 6 plunges into the art of fostering prospects using ChatGPT-4, which is an essential step in the grand marketing dance. Generating leads, or attracting potential customers, is akin to inviting people to a party - the more appealing the invitation, the more guests show up. ChatGPT-4 can be the host with the most, charming potential customers and transforming them into guests. This chapter will reveal how ChatGPT-4, with its charismatic features, can help you craft irresistible landing pages, akin to invitations, that convert casual visitors into eager attendees. Whether your goal is to grow an email list, boost sales, or expand your customer family, ChatGPT-4 can lead you to your dance floor.

Creating Engaging Landing Pages with ChatGPT-4

Moving from the realm of YouTube, let's now set our sights on another powerful tool in your marketing arsenal: landing pages. These are standalone web pages, designed for a single focused objective. Picture them as the stage on which you make your sales pitch. But how can ChatGPT-4 help in creating engaging landing pages? Let's dive right in.

To begin, ChatGPT-4 can aid in crafting compelling headlines and subheadlines. These elements are the first things visitors see, and their quality can make or break a user's decision to stay on your page. The AI can analyze successful landing pages, identify patterns, and use these insights to generate compelling headlines that grab attention and spark interest.

Next, we have the body text. This is where you lay out the details of your offer and make your sales pitch. ChatGPT-4 can assist in writing persuasive copy that clearly communicates the value of your offer and compels visitors to take action. Moreover, the AI can ensure that your copy is concise, engaging, and free of errors, helping to maintain a professional image.

Let's not forget the call-to-action (CTA), the part of the landing page that prompts users to take some action, like signing up for a newsletter or purchasing a product. ChatGPT-4 can generate compelling CTAs that drive users to act. Remember, a well-crafted CTA can be the difference between a bounce and a conversion.

To add a cherry on top, ChatGPT-4 can help with A/B testing of your landing pages. This process involves comparing two versions of a page to see which one performs better. The AI can generate alternative headlines, body text, and CTAs for testing, providing valuable insights into what resonates best with your audience.

Here's a recap of the key points from this section:

1. ChatGPT-4 can assist in creating engaging landing pages by crafting compelling headlines, writing persuasive body copy, generating effective CTAs, and aiding in A/B testing.

2. The AI can analyze successful landing pages to identify patterns and insights that it can use in creating your own landing pages.

3. ChatGPT-4 can help maintain a professional image by ensuring your landing page copy is concise, engaging, and free of errors.

4. The AI can be used for A/B testing, generating alternative elements for your landing pages to see which ones resonate best with your audience.

Next, we're ready to embark on our next journey: "ChatGPT-4 for Sales Emails and Follow-ups." We've seen how AI can enhance our web presence, but how can it help in our email marketing efforts?

ChatGPT-4 for Sales Emails and Follow-ups

With our minds still buzzing from the exploration of creating engaging landing pages, let's direct our attention to another crucial element of business marketing: sales emails and follow-ups. Picture this: you've managed to get a potential customer's attention. They've expressed interest, and now you've got to keep the ball rolling. This is where sales emails and follow-ups come into the picture, and where ChatGPT-4 can lend a helping hand.

When it comes to sales emails, it's all about communication. And what is ChatGPT-4 known for, if not its ability to generate human-like text? With ChatGPT-4, you can create engaging, personalized emails that can resonate with your potential customers. Whether you're reaching out for the first time or following up on a previous interaction, ChatGPT-4 can help craft the perfect message.

Beyond crafting engaging emails, ChatGPT-4 can help optimize the timing and frequency of your messages. By analyzing past interactions and customer behaviors, the AI can suggest the optimal times to send emails and the right frequency to avoid overwhelming your potential customers.

Another area where ChatGPT-4 can offer significant value is in crafting follow-up emails. Follow-ups are essential in sales, but they can be tricky. You want to remind your potential customers of your product or service without coming off as annoying or pushy. With ChatGPT-4, you can craft follow-up emails that strike the right balance, keeping your prospects engaged without putting them off.

Finally, ChatGPT-4 can assist with tracking and analyzing the effectiveness of your sales emails. By generating alternative versions of your emails, the AI can help you conduct A/B testing to determine what works best for your audience. This kind of data-driven approach can make your email marketing more effective and improve your overall conversion rates.

Let's recap the key points we've covered in this section:

1. ChatGPT-4 can help create engaging, personalized sales emails that resonate with your potential customers.

2. The AI can optimize the timing and frequency of your emails based on past interactions and customer behaviors.

3. ChatGPT-4 can assist in crafting follow-up emails that keep prospects engaged without being overly pushy.

4. The AI can also aid in tracking and analyzing the effectiveness of your sales emails, enabling a data-driven approach to improve your email marketing and conversion rates.

In the next section, we'll dive into "Optimizing Conversion Rates with ChatGPT-4". We've seen how AI can be used to enhance our sales emails and follow-ups. But how can it help us optimize the conversion rates, the holy grail of marketing?

Optimizing Conversion Rates with ChatGPT-4

As we continue our exploration of artificial intelligence in business marketing, let's pause to consider a crucial metric that no marketer can afford to ignore: conversion rates. A conversion rate is the percentage of visitors to your website who complete a desired goal out of the total number of visitors. For instance, if your goal is for visitors to make a purchase, then the conversion rate would be the percentage of visitors who make a purchase. Let's explore how ChatGPT-4 can help optimize these all-important conversion rates.

Imagine your website as a party. Your visitors are the guests, and the host's job—your job—is to guide them towards the action you want them to take. This is where ChatGPT-4 comes into play, as the perfect co-host. By using its language model capabilities, the AI can analyze the text on your site, understand the objective, and suggest improvements to increase your conversion rates.

One way ChatGPT-4 can help is by creating engaging and persuasive copy. As we've seen in previous chapters, the language model is adept at crafting compelling text. By harnessing this capability, you can enhance your product descriptions, blog posts, and landing pages, making them more likely to convert visitors into customers.

Another way ChatGPT-4 can boost conversion rates is by improving your calls-to-action (CTAs). These are the prompts that tell your visitors what action to take next. A well-crafted CTA can greatly increase the likelihood of a visitor taking the desired action, and ChatGPT-4 can help create CTAs that are both compelling and perfectly suited to your audience.

Furthermore, ChatGPT-4 can assist with personalization, a strategy that involves tailoring your website and marketing materials to individual users based on their behaviors and preferences. By analyzing user data, the AI can generate personalized product recommendations, emails, and more, all of which can lead to higher conversion rates.

Finally, ChatGPT-4 can help with A/B testing, a method of comparing two versions of a webpage or other marketing asset to see which one performs better. By generating alternative versions of your site's text, ChatGPT-4 can enable you to conduct robust A/B testing and make data-driven decisions to optimize your conversion rates.

Let's summarize the key points from this section:

1. ChatGPT-4 can help optimize conversion rates by creating engaging and persuasive copy, improving your CTAs, assisting with personalization, and aiding in A/B testing.

2. The AI's language model capabilities can enhance your site's text to make it more compelling and conversion-friendly.

3. ChatGPT-4 can generate personalized marketing materials based on user data, leading to higher conversion rates.

4. The AI can assist with A/B testing by creating alternative versions of your site's text, enabling you to make data-driven decisions to optimize your conversion rates.

Having explored how ChatGPT-4 can optimize conversion rates, we are now ready to delve into our next topic:

"Maximizing Profits with ChatGPT-4". We've seen how AI can boost conversions, but how can it help increase profits?

Chapter 7: Maximizing Profits with ChatGPT-4

Chapter 7 delves into the ways in which businesses can use AI to maximize their profits. ChatGPT-4 is a powerful tool that can help businesses optimize their marketing strategies, improve customer engagement, and increase conversions. By using ChatGPT-4 for market research and analysis, businesses can gain valuable insights into customer behavior and preferences, allowing them to tailor their marketing efforts to better meet the needs of their target audience. Additionally, ChatGPT-4 can be used to generate personalized content that speaks directly to individual customers, increasing the likelihood of conversion. However, it's important to note that AI is not a silver bullet, and businesses must still rely on human expertise and creativity to succeed. By using ChatGPT-4 in conjunction with other marketing tools and techniques, businesses can create a powerful and effective marketing strategy that drives real results.

Using ChatGPT-4 for Market Research and Analysis

Fresh from the exciting journey of optimizing conversion rates, let's now pivot to another integral piece of the business puzzle: market research and analysis. Imagine stepping into a vast, buzzing market with stalls as far as the eye can see. Each stall represents a segment of your potential market, and each customer, a trend or a preference. Your task is to make sense of this bustling scene, identify the opportunities, and understand the risks. This task can be daunting, but not when you have ChatGPT-4 by your side.

ChatGPT-4 can be a game-changer in your market research efforts. Picture an AI assistant that can sift through tons of data, spot patterns, and deliver insights in a language you understand. ChatGPT-4 can analyze data from diverse sources, such as social media conversations, customer reviews, and industry reports, to give you a clearer picture of the market landscape.

This mighty AI tool can also help identify and track emerging trends. By continuously scanning and analyzing online data, ChatGPT-4 can spot shifts in consumer behavior or new trends before they become mainstream. Think of it as having your finger constantly on the pulse of the market.

Moreover, ChatGPT-4 can offer valuable insights into your competition. The AI can analyze your competitors' online presence, track their product developments, and even gauge customer sentiment towards them. This competitive intelligence can help you stay one step ahead in the game.

Last but not least, ChatGPT-4 can assist in customer segmentation. By analyzing customer data, the AI can group your customers into distinct segments based on their behaviors, preferences, or needs. This segmentation can help you tailor your marketing strategies to better meet the needs of different customer groups.

To summarize the key points we've covered in this section:

1. ChatGPT-4 can analyze data from various sources to deliver market insights in a comprehensible manner.

2. The AI can identify and track emerging trends by continuously scanning and analyzing online data.

3. ChatGPT-4 can provide competitive intelligence by analyzing your competitors' online presence, product developments, and customer sentiment.

4. The AI can assist in customer segmentation, helping you tailor your marketing strategies to different customer groups.

Our next stop on this journey is "Price Optimization with ChatGPT-4". Price is a critical factor in the buying decision. But how do you set the right price that maximizes profits while still appealing to customers?

Price Optimization with ChatGPT-4

We delved into the world of market research, an exploration made all the more thrilling with the aid of ChatGPT-4. Now, with insights in hand and a clearer understanding of your customer segments and competitors, let's turn our attention to a crucial aspect of any business: price optimization.

Price optimization is the process of setting the right price for a product or service. This isn't about simply covering your costs and slapping on a margin. No, it's more nuanced than that. It involves understanding your customers' willingness to pay, your competition, market conditions, and your business objectives. And this is where ChatGPT-4 shows its prowess.

ChatGPT-4 can analyze vast amounts of data to help determine the price that maximizes profits without alienating customers. It can analyze historical sales data, consumer behavior, and market trends to determine the optimal price point for your offerings. And the beauty of it is that it can do this for each of your customer segments, product categories, and even individual products.

With ChatGPT-4, you can also implement dynamic pricing. This is where prices fluctuate based on real-time supply and demand. For example, if the AI detects an increased interest in a product (based on web traffic, social media buzz, etc.), it could suggest a slight price increase to capitalize on this demand. Conversely, if a product is not moving as expected, it could recommend a timely price reduction.

Another exciting application of ChatGPT-4 is in price testing. The AI can simulate different pricing scenarios and predict their impact on sales and profits. This can provide valuable insights before you implement any price changes in the real world.

To encapsulate the salient points of this section:

1. ChatGPT-4 can analyze various data to help determine the price point that maximizes profits without alienating customers.

2. The AI can facilitate dynamic pricing, where prices fluctuate based on real-time supply and demand.

3. ChatGPT-4 can simulate different pricing scenarios and predict their impact on sales and profits.

Next, we'll be setting our sights on "Scaling Your Business with ChatGPT-4". As exciting as starting a business is, scaling it to new heights can be equally, if not more, exhilarating. With our friend ChatGPT-4, we'll explore how to grow your business sustainably while maintaining quality and customer satisfaction.

Scaling Your Business with ChatGPT-4

After journeying through the landscapes of pricing optimization, we're now going to switch gears and look at how we can take the engine of your business and supercharge it for growth. The term 'scaling your business' can often sound daunting, but with the right strategies, and with ChatGPT-4 at your side, it can be a thrilling adventure of expansion and evolution.

Scaling a business involves growing its capacity to handle an increase in sales, workload, and overall demand. This isn't just about getting bigger; it's about getting better. It's about increasing output without compromising on quality or customer experience. This is where ChatGPT-4 can provide significant assistance.

When it comes to customer service and support, ChatGPT-4 can handle a large volume of queries, requests, and complaints in real-time, ensuring that your customers always feel heard and valued. And it can do this 24/7, across different channels and in multiple languages, providing a seamless customer experience as your business expands geographically.

In terms of operations and logistics, ChatGPT-4 can analyze patterns in your data to streamline your processes, optimize your inventory, and even predict potential bottlenecks or disruptions. It can also help automate routine tasks, freeing up your team to focus on strategic initiatives and creative problem-solving.

For marketing and sales, ChatGPT-4 can help tailor your messaging for different customer segments and optimize your campaigns for greater reach and conversion. It can also aid in identifying new market opportunities and assessing potential risks.

Now, let's distill the key points from this section:

1. ChatGPT-4 can handle a large volume of customer service interactions, providing a consistent and seamless experience as your business grows.

2. The AI can analyze operational data to optimize processes, predict issues, and automate routine tasks.

3. ChatGPT-4 can tailor your marketing and sales efforts for different customer segments and help identify new market opportunities.

We now prepare to step into a new realm - "PART IV: Looking Ahead: The Future of AI in Business". The promise of AI is expansive, and as we move forward, it's essential to keep our eyes on the horizon. How will AI continue to shape business practices? What are the ethical considerations we must bear in mind? And how can we prepare for this future? These are just some of the questions we'll explore, so stay tuned for an enlightening exploration of what lies ahead.

PART IV:
Looking Ahead: The Future of AI in Business

Chapter 8:
The Promise of GPT-5: An Early Look

This chapter explores the exciting possibilities of the next generation of AI, GPT-5. GPT-5 is the next evolutionary step in AI, and it's sparking conversations and theories across the globe. GPT-5 is expected to have enhanced text generation capabilities, improved context understanding, and advanced data analysis and prediction capabilities. These potential features could revolutionize decision-making in businesses and transform the landscape of business marketing. However, it's important to note that GPT-5 is still in development, and it may be some time before it is released to the public. Nonetheless, businesses must stay up-to-date on the latest developments in AI to remain competitive in the rapidly evolving field of marketing. By embracing the promise of GPT-5 and other AI technologies, businesses can create a powerful and effective marketing strategy that drives real results.

The Anticipation Surrounding GPT-5

As we continue our journey into the future of AI, it's impossible to ignore the mounting anticipation surrounding the next evolutionary step: GPT-5. This yet-to-be-released AI model is sparking conversations and theories across the globe, as we all wonder what new capabilities it could bring to the table.

The success of GPT-4 lies in its ability to understand and generate human-like text based on the context provided to it. But as we look forward to GPT-5, the question becomes: how can this technology be improved? What untapped potential lies in the horizon, waiting to be explored?

One of the areas where we anticipate significant advancements is in the understanding of nuanced human language and emotions. If GPT-5 can better grasp the subtleties of our language, its ability to interact with users and provide relevant responses could greatly improve, making it an even more powerful tool for businesses.

Another possible enhancement lies in the realm of 'transfer learning', a concept in AI where a model trained on one task can apply its knowledge to a different but related task. If GPT-5 can master this, it could mean an AI that can adapt more swiftly and effectively, learning new tasks with less data and fewer instructions.

Further, there's the prospect of even more sophisticated data analysis. If GPT-5 can dive deeper into data, recognize patterns more accurately, and make more precise predictions, it could revolutionize industries from healthcare to finance to marketing and beyond.

To summarize, here are the key points we've touched on regarding the anticipation surrounding GPT-5:

1. Enhanced understanding of nuanced human language and emotions could make GPT-5 an even more effective communication tool.

2. Potential improvements in transfer learning could lead to an AI that can adapt and learn new tasks more efficiently.

3. The possibility of more sophisticated data analysis and prediction could have far-reaching impacts across numerous industries.

As we look ahead, there's no doubt that the potential of GPT-5 is electrifying. But what exactly might these new features and capabilities look like? In the next section, "Potential Features and Capabilities of GPT-5", we'll delve into the hypotheticals, exploring the possibilities that could soon become realities. So, buckle up, and let's continue this exciting exploration into the future of AI.

Potential Features and Capabilities of GPT-5

As we shift our gaze to the yet-uncharted territory of GPT-5, we're presented with a fascinating playground of potential features and capabilities. While we can't predict with certainty what these will be, we can certainly engage in some informed speculation, based on the trajectory of the technology thus far.

One of the most anticipated features of GPT-5 is an enhanced ability to understand and generate text based on more abstract and complex concepts. If GPT-4 can generate a paragraph from a simple prompt, imagine GPT-5 being able to craft a detailed report from a set of bullet points, or a coherent story from a random collection of ideas.

We can also envision improvements in the realm of context understanding. GPT-4 can understand and respond based on the context provided in the immediate conversation. However, GPT-5 might be able to consider larger conversational context, historical interactions, or even global trends and events to provide even more relevant and insightful responses.

Another potential upgrade could be in the area of 'generative adversarial networks' (GANs), a type of AI model where two neural networks contest with each other to achieve better results. In the context of GPT-5, this could mean a model that can generate text and simultaneously evaluate and refine its own outputs, leading to more accurate and high-quality content.

Lastly, GPT-5 could bring advancements in data analysis and prediction. Imagine an AI that can not only analyze complex data sets, but also predict future trends, identify potential issues, and suggest innovative solutions. The potential benefits for businesses are astronomical.

Here are the key points we've imagined for GPT-5:

1. Enhanced text generation based on abstract and complex concepts could lead to more sophisticated content creation.

2. Improved context understanding could result in more relevant and insightful interactions.

3. The use of generative adversarial networks could lead to self-refining AI models that produce more accurate outputs.

4. Advanced data analysis and prediction capabilities could revolutionize decision-making in businesses.

With these potential features in mind, it's time to turn our attention to how they might be applied in a business context. In the next section, "Imagining GPT-5 in Business Marketing", we'll explore how these hypothetical capabilities of GPT-5 could transform the landscape of business marketing. Prepare to step into a world where the boundary between human and AI-generated content becomes even more blurred.

Imagining GPT-5 in Business Marketing

As we venture into the realm of possibilities with GPT-5 in the business marketing landscape, let's consider a world where the line between human and machine becomes increasingly indistinguishable. This may sound like the stuff of science fiction, but given the trajectory of AI development, it's closer to reality than you might think.

Picture a marketing landscape where businesses utilize GPT-5's advanced text generation capabilities to craft customized marketing messages for individual consumers, based on their unique preferences and past interactions. These messages could be so well-tailored and human-like that customers feel as though they're interacting with a personal marketing assistant rather than an AI.

With improved context understanding, GPT-5 could analyze customer behavior across multiple platforms and channels, providing businesses with a comprehensive understanding of their customers' needs, preferences, and behaviors. This could lead to an unprecedented level of personalization in marketing strategies, making customers feel truly understood and valued.

Imagine using GPT-5's advanced data analysis and prediction capabilities to forecast market trends, customer behavior, and even the success of various marketing strategies. Businesses could identify potential opportunities and challenges well in advance, allowing them to adjust their marketing strategies proactively and stay ahead of the competition.

Finally, with the potential self-refining abilities through generative adversarial networks, GPT-5 could continuously improve its marketing strategies based on feedback and performance. This could lead to increasingly effective marketing campaigns, with the AI learning and adapting in real-time.

Here are the key points from our exploration of GPT-5 in business marketing:

1. Advanced text generation could enable highly personalized marketing messages.

2. Improved context understanding could lead to a comprehensive understanding of customers' needs and behaviors.

3. Enhanced data analysis and prediction could allow for proactive adjustment of marketing strategies.

4. Self-refining abilities could result in continuously improving marketing campaigns.

Having imagined the future possibilities of GPT-5 in business marketing, it's important to not lose sight of the ethical considerations and best practices in navigating the AI landscape. In the next chapter, "Navigating the AI Landscape: Ethics, Regulations, and Best Practices", we'll delve into these essential aspects, ensuring that as we stride into the future of AI in business, we do so with responsibility, integrity, and a clear understanding of the rules of the game.

Chapter 9:
Navigating the AI Landscape: Ethics, Regulations, and Best Practices

Chapter 9 explores the ethical implications of AI and the importance of navigating AI regulations in business. As AI continues to evolve and become more integrated into our daily lives, it's crucial that we take a moment to reflect on the ethical implications of this technology. AI has the potential to transform the way we live and work, but it also raises important questions about privacy, security, and accountability. Additionally, businesses must navigate a complex landscape of regulations and best practices to ensure that they are using AI in a responsible and ethical manner. By understanding the ethical implications of AI and staying up-to-date on the latest regulations and best practices, businesses can create a powerful and effective marketing strategy that drives real results while also upholding ethical standards.

Understanding the Ethical Implications of AI

As we proceed on this journey through the landscape of artificial intelligence, it is crucial that we take a moment to pause and reflect on the ethical implications. After all, we're not just in the business of pushing boundaries; we're also responsible for ensuring that our advancements respect the fundamental principles of fairness, privacy, and transparency.

In the world of AI, ethical considerations are not just afterthoughts—they are foundational elements. Consider the issue of bias. AI systems learn from the data they're fed, and if that data is biased, the AI's outputs can be biased too. For example, if an AI system is trained on data that reflects gender or racial bias, it could inadvertently perpetuate those biases. It's therefore essential to ensure that the data used to train AI systems like GPT-4 or GPT-5 is as unbiased and representative as possible.

Next, let's talk about privacy. With AI's ability to gather, analyze, and learn from vast amounts of data comes the responsibility to protect that data. It's crucial to respect the privacy rights of individuals and to use data responsibly and transparently.

Lastly, there's the issue of transparency. AI is a powerful tool, but it can also be a black box, with complex algorithms that are difficult to understand. To build trust, businesses must strive for transparency, explaining how their AI systems work and how they make decisions.

And now, let's summarize the key points we've discussed:

1. Bias: Ensure that the data used to train AI systems is unbiased and representative.

2. Privacy: Respect the privacy rights of individuals and use data responsibly and transparently.

3. Transparency: Strive to explain how AI systems work and how they make decisions.

Having gained a deeper understanding of the ethical considerations in AI, it's time to explore another vital area - the regulatory landscape. In the next section, "Navigating AI Regulations in Business," we'll guide you through the rules, regulations, and guidelines that govern the use of AI in business. Remember, being savvy about AI isn't just about harnessing its power—it's also about understanding its limits.

Navigating AI Regulations in Business

As we pivot from our discussion on ethics, it's time to turn the spotlight on the regulatory landscape of artificial intelligence in business. These rules, guidelines, and legal frameworks aren't just red tape—they serve as boundaries that protect us while enabling innovation to flourish. It's like having guardrails on a high-speed freeway; they don't impede progress, but they ensure our journey is safe.

The world of AI regulation is still evolving, with governments and international organizations working to keep pace with the rapid advances in technology. These regulations often focus on data protection, AI transparency, and fairness. For instance, the European Union's General Data Protection Regulation (GDPR) has stringent rules on how personal data can be used, including by AI systems. Violations of these regulations can result in hefty fines, not to mention damage to a company's reputation.

Understanding the regulatory environment is not just about compliance, it's also about opportunity. By staying ahead of the curve and understanding emerging regulations, businesses can position themselves as industry leaders, turning regulatory compliance into a competitive advantage. Think of it as a form of risk management: By understanding the rules, you can better navigate the landscape and avoid potential pitfalls.

In the United States, regulations are typically sector-specific. For instance, AI applications in healthcare must comply with the Health Insurance Portability and Accountability Act (HIPAA), which protects patient data. On the other hand, AI used in financial services is subject to regulations like the Dodd-Frank Act, which aims to promote financial stability.

Now, let's summarize the key points from this section:

1. The regulatory landscape for AI is evolving, with rules focusing on data protection, transparency, and fairness.

2. Regulatory compliance can be turned into a competitive advantage by positioning your business as an industry leader.

3. Regulations are typically sector-specific, with different rules for different industries.

As we look ahead to our next section, "Best Practices for Implementing AI in Your Business," we will transition from understanding to action. Now that we've covered the foundational ethics and regulations of AI, we can explore how to effectively implement these systems in your business. As you'll soon see, a successful AI strategy isn't just about technology—it's also about people, processes, and purpose.

Best Practices for Implementing AI in Your Business

Welcome to the "how-to" section on implementing AI in your business, where we take our knowledge and insights from previous chapters and apply them to practical steps. Let's think of this as building a house: We've laid the foundation with understanding AI, we've set up the framework with ethical considerations and regulatory guidelines, and now it's time to start construction.

The first step in implementing AI is to clearly define your goals. What problems are you hoping to solve? What tasks can be automated? The answers to these questions will guide your AI strategy. It's like going on a road trip—you need to know your destination before you can plan the route.

Next, gather your team. Successful AI implementation requires collaboration between various teams in your organization—from IT professionals who will handle the technical aspects to HR representatives who will manage potential changes in roles and responsibilities. This isn't a one-person show; it's more like an ensemble cast, with everyone playing their part to bring the story to life.

With your team in place, you can start the process of selecting and implementing your AI system. This involves choosing the right AI model that fits your needs, training the model with relevant data, testing it to ensure it's working correctly, and then deploying it. It's akin to preparing a meal —you select your recipe (AI model), gather your ingredients (data), cook your meal (train the model), taste it to make sure it's good (testing), and then serve it (deployment).

Finally, remember that implementing AI is not a one-time event but an ongoing process. Regular monitoring and maintenance are required to ensure the system remains effective and relevant. Just like a car needs regular servicing to stay in top condition, your AI system needs consistent tuning and adjustments to perform at its best.

To recap, here are the key points:

1. Define clear goals for your AI implementation.

2. Form a collaborative team from various departments.

3. Select and implement the appropriate AI model.

4. Regularly monitor and maintain your AI system.

Looking ahead to our final chapter, "Embracing the AI Revolution in Business," we'll reflect on our journey and look towards the future. As we've seen, AI is not just a trend—it's a transformative force that's reshaping the business landscape. And as we move forward, embracing this revolution will be key to staying competitive and driving growth. So, buckle up—it's time to embrace the AI revolution in business.

Chapter 10:
Conclusion: Embracing the AI Revolution in Business

Chapter 10 concludes our fascinating expedition through the AI-infused marketing landscape. This chapter will offer a moment of reflection on our exploration of ChatGPT-4 and its marketing applications, as well as ponder the broader implications of AI on the marketing industry. We'll also gaze into the crystal ball to envision the future of AI in marketing. Whether you're a marketer, business owner, or just intrigued by the union of AI and marketing, this chapter will offer nuggets of wisdom and thought-provoking insights to help you navigate this rapidly evolving terrain.

Reflecting on the Journey: From GPT-4 to GPT-5

We have journeyed together through the world of AI, from the birth of GPT-4 to the anticipation of GPT-5. It's been like a hike up a mountain, where each step brings a fresh perspective and a new understanding of the landscape below.

We've seen how GPT-4 revolutionized business marketing, acting as a powerful tool for creating content, engaging with customers, and analyzing data. It's like a Swiss Army knife in the world of AI—versatile, adaptable, and ever-reliable. And it's opened doors to opportunities that were previously unimaginable, much like a key that unlocks a treasure chest of possibilities.

As we stand at the precipice of the launch of GPT-5, we look back on the path we've walked and forward to the journey yet to come. If GPT-4 is the Swiss Army knife, then GPT-5 could be seen as the entire toolbox—promising even more functionality, adaptability, and potential for businesses. And just as a toolbox allows us to tackle a wider range of tasks, we anticipate GPT-5 expanding the horizons of what's possible in business marketing.

But let's not forget that with great power comes great responsibility. As AI becomes increasingly sophisticated, the ethical implications and regulatory considerations become ever more important. Think of it as a powerful car: The faster it can go, the more carefully we need to drive and the more important the rules of the road become.

So, as we look forward to GPT-5, we do so with a sense of excitement and caution, much like a child on the night before a big trip: excited for the adventure ahead but aware of the need for preparation and safety.

Key points from our journey:

1. GPT-4 revolutionized business marketing with its versatile capabilities.

2. The anticipation of GPT-5 promises even more functionality and potential.

3. With the advancement of AI, ethical implications and regulatory considerations become increasingly important.

As we move into the next section "Preparing Your Business for the Future of AI," we'll equip you with the insights and tools you need to navigate this rapidly evolving landscape. We'll explore how to future-proof your business and ensure that as AI continues to advance, your business advances with it. It's like packing for a journey—you need to be prepared for the road ahead, and we're here to help you pack your suitcase.

Preparing Your Business for the Future of AI

As we stand on the brink of a new era in artificial intelligence, it's imperative that we prepare our businesses to ride this wave of change, just as a sailor readies their ship for a voyage at sea. The future of AI is not a distant shore, but a horizon that is rapidly approaching. Therefore, our businesses need to be agile, adaptable, and open to the winds of innovation.

First and foremost, this preparation involves fostering a culture of continuous learning within our organizations. Think of this as planting a garden: the seeds we sow today in terms of learning and development will blossom into the skills and knowledge we need to navigate the AI landscape of tomorrow. Encourage your teams to learn about AI, to experiment with it, and to integrate it into their daily work. Remember, a garden of continuous learning requires constant nurturing and attention.

Next, we need to invest in the right infrastructure and tools. Just as a carpenter needs a solid workbench and a set of high-quality tools, businesses need robust technological infrastructure to support the implementation of AI. This could involve upgrading systems, investing in new software, or partnering with AI service providers. It's like setting up a home—it requires careful planning, investment, and the right materials.

Moreover, we must not lose sight of the human element. AI is a powerful tool, but it cannot replace the creativity, empathy, and intuition that humans bring to the table. It's like a paintbrush in the hands of an artist: the brush can create beautiful strokes, but the vision and creativity come from the artist. As such, we need to strike a balance between AI and human input, leveraging the strengths of each to create a harmonious symphony of productivity and innovation.

Finally, in preparing for the future of AI, we must also consider the ethical and regulatory implications. This is akin to driving a car: we must understand the rules of the road, respect the rights of other drivers, and drive responsibly. As AI becomes more integrated into our businesses, we must ensure that it is used in a manner that is ethical, respectful, and in compliance with all relevant laws and regulations.

Key points for preparing your business for the future of AI:

1. Foster a culture of continuous learning.

2. Invest in the right infrastructure and tools.

3. Balance AI and human input.

4. Consider the ethical and regulatory implications.

Now, as we venture into our final section, "Final Thoughts and Next Steps," we'll reflect on the journey we've undertaken together, and chart out the course for the road ahead. Like a captain plotting a course on a map, we'll help you navigate the waters of AI and steer your business towards a future of growth and innovation.

Final Thoughts and Next Steps

Just as every great journey has a starting point and a destination, we have journeyed together through the landscape of AI, exploring its capabilities, potential, and implications for your business. As we reach the end of this particular journey, it's time to look back at what we've learned, and more importantly, look forward to what's next.

Our exploration began with understanding the capabilities of GPT-4 and how it could be applied to business marketing. Think of this as learning to play a musical instrument. We began with the basics, understanding the instrument, learning the scales, and playing simple melodies. Then, we expanded our repertoire, learning to play complex pieces and even composing our own.

Similarly, we began with the basics of GPT-4, understanding its capabilities and limitations, and then learned how to apply it effectively in business marketing. Like a well-composed melody, when applied effectively, GPT-4 can harmonize with your business strategies and amplify your marketing efforts.

Next, we ventured into the realm of possibilities, imagining the future with GPT-5. This was akin to peering into a crystal ball and trying to discern the shapes and shadows within. We discussed the potential advancements and capabilities of GPT-5, and how they could revolutionize business marketing.

Then, we navigated the complex waters of AI ethics and regulations, understanding their importance and relevance to your business. This was like learning to drive; understanding the rules of the road, respecting other drivers, and driving responsibly.

Finally, we discussed best practices for implementing AI in your business and preparing your business for the future of AI. This was like learning to cook; gathering the right ingredients, following the recipe, and adding your own unique touch.

As we conclude this journey, remember that learning about AI is not a destination, but a journey of continuous exploration and discovery. Each step you take in understanding and integrating AI into your business is a step towards future success.

Here are the key points we've covered:

1. Understanding and applying GPT-4 in business marketing.

2. Imagining the future with GPT-5.

3. Navigating AI ethics and regulations.

4. Best practices for implementing AI in your business.

5. Preparing your business for the future of AI.

Just like the ending of a great book or the finale of a symphony, our journey through the world of AI and business marketing does not end here. Instead, it serves as a prelude to the great possibilities and adventures that await us. As we close this chapter, I encourage you to take the insights and knowledge you've gained and use them as a compass, guiding you through the exciting landscape of AI in business. Remember, the future is not a distant horizon but an exciting adventure that begins with a single step. And so, with anticipation and excitement, we step into the future, eager to embrace the wonders that AI holds for our businesses.

Part V:
Appendices

Appendix A:
Possible uses for ChatGPT-4 in Business

1. Customer Service: Answering FAQs, assisting in troubleshooting, handling complaints, or guiding customers through processes.

2. Sales Assistance: Providing product information, recommending products, or assisting in sales transactions.

3. Content Creation: Drafting blog posts, creating social media content, or generating marketing copy.

4. Data Analysis: Interpreting and explaining complex data sets.

5. Training: Assisting in the development of training materials or acting as an interactive training tool.

6. Personal Assistant: Scheduling appointments, sending reminders, or organizing tasks.

7. Market Research: Gathering and analyzing customer feedback or sentiments.

8. Technical Support: Guiding users through technical troubleshooting.

9. Product Development: Generating new ideas or brainstorming for product improvement.

10. Crisis Management: Assisting in drafting communication during crisis situations.

11. Translation: Translating business documents or conversations.

12. Email Drafting: Assisting in drafting professional emails.

13. Social Media Monitoring: Analyzing sentiments and trends from social media posts.

14. Team Communication: Acting as an interface for project management tools to facilitate team communication.

15. Hiring: Screening candidates, scheduling interviews, and answering candidate queries.

16. Business Forecasting: Helping interpret trends and data for business forecasting.

17. Legal Assistance: Assisting in understanding legal terminology or drafting legal documents.

18. Accessibility: Assisting employees or customers with disabilities by providing alternative text or voice-based interaction.

19. Internal Knowledge Base: Answering employee queries about company policies or procedures.

20. Onboarding: Guiding new employees through company processes and systems.

21. Event Planning: Assisting in scheduling, sending invites, and coordinating events.

22. Public Relations: Drafting press releases or handling PR queries.

23. Inventory Management: Assisting in tracking and managing inventory.

24. E-commerce Chatbots: Assisting customers on e-commerce platforms.

25. Ideation: Brainstorming business strategies or creative ideas.

26. Meeting Facilitation: Assisting in scheduling, setting agendas, and recording minutes for meetings.

27. Document Review: Assisting in reviewing and summarizing lengthy documents.

28. Industry Research: Summarizing news or trends in a specific industry.

29. Financial Advice: Providing basic financial advice or guidance based on user queries.

30. Sentiment Analysis: Understanding customer sentiment from reviews, social media posts, or other feedback.

31. Brand Management: Assisting in maintaining brand voice across multiple channels of communication.

32. Business Intelligence: Assisting in the interpretation of business data to inform decision-making.

33. Competitive Analysis: Summarizing news or trends about competitors.

34. Virtual Tours: Guiding customers through virtual tours of properties or facilities.

35. Content Curation: Assisting in curating relevant content for newsletters or social media.

36. SEO Optimization: Providing recommendations to optimize content for search engine visibility.

37. Risk Management: Assisting in the identification and assessment of business risks.

38. Procurement: Assisting in tracking orders, managing suppliers, or other procurement tasks.

39. Wellness Program: Providing mental health support or wellness tips to employees.

40. Learning & Development: Facilitating personalized learning paths for employees.

41. Invoice Queries: Answering queries related to invoices or payments.

42. Sustainability Initiatives: Assisting in communicating and tracking sustainability initiatives.

43. Quality Control: Assisting in monitoring quality across various business processes.

44. Corporate Social Responsibility: Assisting in managing and communicating CSR activities.

45. Travel Management: Assisting employees in planning and booking business travel.

46. R&D: Assisting in research and development processes.

47. Ethical Compliance: Assisting in maintaining and monitoring ethical compliance across business operations.

48. Supply Chain Management: Assisting in managing and optimizing the supply chain.

49. Diversity & Inclusion: Assisting in promoting and tracking diversity and inclusion initiatives.

50. Real Estate: Assisting customers in property search and providing property details.

51. Sustainability Reporting: Assisting in compiling and reporting on sustainability initiatives.

52. Employee Engagement: Assisting in surveys, polls, or other engagement activities.

53. Crisis Communication: Assisting in crafting messages during a crisis or emergency.

54. Investor Relations: Assisting in drafting financial reports, press releases, and communication with shareholders.

55. Regulatory Compliance: Assisting in understanding and maintaining regulatory compliance.

56. Project Management: Assisting in tracking project progress, identifying risks, and facilitating communication.

57. Knowledge Management: Assisting in organizing and retrieving knowledge within the organization.

58. Performance Management: Assisting in tracking and reporting employee performance metrics.

59. Change Management: Assisting in communicating changes in business processes or strategies.

60. HR Policy Communication: Assisting in explaining and answering queries about HR policies.

61. Fraud Detection: Assisting in identifying potential fraudulent activities or inconsistencies.

62. Contract Management: Assisting in managing and maintaining business contracts.

63. Corporate Governance: Assisting in ensuring adherence to corporate governance principles.

64. Diversity Training: Assisting in providing training on diversity and inclusion.

65. Environmental Impact Assessment: Assisting in assessing and reporting environmental impact.

66. ESG Reporting: Assisting in compiling and reporting on Environmental, Social, and Governance (ESG) factors.

67. Business Continuity Planning: Assisting in planning for business continuity in case of emergencies.

68. IT Asset Management: Assisting in tracking and managing IT assets within the organization.

69. Software Development: Assisting in generating code or debugging software issues.

70. User Experience Testing: Assisting in conducting user experience tests and gathering feedback.

71. Safety Compliance: Assisting in maintaining and checking safety compliance in relevant industries.

72. Energy Management: Assisting in tracking and optimizing energy usage in business operations.

73. Disaster Recovery Planning: Assisting in planning and communication for disaster recovery.

74. Facility Management: Assisting in managing and maintaining business facilities.

75. Operational Efficiency: Assisting in identifying bottlenecks and suggesting improvements for operational efficiency.

76. Peer Recognition: Assisting in facilitating peer recognition programs in workplaces.

77. Business Planning: Assisting in creating and revising business plans based on user inputs.

78. Talent Management: Assisting in identifying and nurturing high-potential employees.

79. Digital Asset Management: Assisting in organizing, tagging, and retrieving digital assets.

80. Mergers and Acquisitions: Assisting in due diligence processes by summarizing and analyzing relevant documents.

81. Corporate Training: Assisting in creating and delivering corporate training modules.

82. Internal Communications: Assisting in creating newsletters, memos, and other internal communication.

83. Stakeholder Engagement: Assisting in communicating with and managing feedback from stakeholders.

84. Brand Protection: Assisting in monitoring for misuse of a company's brand.

85. Knowledge Sharing: Assisting in facilitating knowledge sharing across different teams or departments.

86. Corporate Culture: Assisting in communicating and reinforcing the company's mission, vision, and values.

87. Event Management: Assisting in planning, coordinating, and promoting corporate events.

88. Lobbying: Assisting in preparing briefing documents, position papers, and other lobbying materials.

89. Business Modelling: Assisting in creating and modifying business models.

90. Scenario Planning: Assisting in creating and analyzing various business scenarios.

91. Product Lifecycle Management: Assisting in managing the lifecycle of products from inception to retirement.

92. Customer Retention: Assisting in identifying at-risk customers and suggesting retention strategies.

93. Pricing Strategy: Assisting in analyzing pricing data and suggesting pricing strategies.

94. Revenue Management: Assisting in optimizing pricing and inventory to maximize revenue.

95. Workforce Planning: Assisting in planning for workforce needs based on business forecasts.

96. Order Management: Assisting in managing customer orders and tracking order status.

97. Export/Import Compliance: Assisting in ensuring compliance with export and import regulations.

98. Cybersecurity: Assisting in educating employees about cybersecurity practices.

99. **Health and Safety:** Assisting in communicating health and safety guidelines and conducting safety checks.

100. Business Ethics: Assisting in communicating and enforcing ethical guidelines within the organization.

www.ingramcontent.com/pod-product-compliance
Lightning Source LLC
Chambersburg PA
CBHW031227050326
40689CB00009B/1499